I0107908

Drunk on Ophelia

by Larry Duncan

SADIE GIRL PRESS

Copyright 2015 Larry Duncan
ISBN-13: 978-0692595800
ISBN-10: 0692595805
Published by Sadie Girl Press
Digital art and photography
by Ken Oddist Jones
Design by Sarah Thursday
Editing and proofreading assistance
by Terry Ann Wright, Raquel
Reyes-Lopez, and Nancy Lynée Woo

Table of Contents

Meaning of Melancholia

Little sister in a vintage coat
the purple of royals
smokes under the sign
of an all-night sushi stand.

From across the street,
a student watches her lean
and wishes for a cigarette
he's never smoked.

Her lipstick bleeds the block sepia.
There is only red
and the print of her leopard
boot, toe raised, heel
grinding at the sidewalk.

There are two empty seats at the bar.
He wishes it was coffee and not cold fish.
Her eyes never leave the tip of her boot.
She wishes herself into an album cover.

He rides the bus
with his books in his lap.
No one else boards
but there's room in the seat.

Exhaust looks sinister
in the red glow of taillights.
She doesn't want to smoke,
but cigarettes are so slender,
a delicate finger between her own.

She lights another.
The night so cold and drunk,
there should be snow,
but it's California
and California doesn't care.

Tienes Que Comer

I dream of burning men
around the kitchen nook at night:
their eggs boiled,
their shadows scorched,
their coffee coal.

"Te amamos," they say,
voices like weight,
like measure and depth.
"Necesitas comida," they say.
The plate is snails,
cracked open and exposed,
slugs without shells,
another kind of gun.

They salt to nothing,
an empty plate.
The meal writhes.

I dream of burning men.
"Te amamos," they say.
"Tienes que comer."

The Standard Enthalpy of Combustion at Work on a Saturday Night

I

Loose bodies spill out of the bars
and into the thick syrup of heat
and hunger bubbling in the street.
Crooked fingers of exhaust,
red in the flare of brake lights,
creep out of tailpipes
and reach for the ankles of lovers,
staggering—arms entangled—
through the sidewalk web of cracks,
drag them over the curb
into the seamless procession
of traffic circling for a space
just a bit closer to home.

They are easy targets.

The Santa Anas are at it again,
driving the arid dreams of the desert
into the chest of the city—
splayed open by the strange
devices of new construction—
on wings of fire and dust.
The traffic lights ache in their spin
and the screens of all the lonely
studios are blown clean,
littering the kitchen sills and tiles
with an indecipherable but familiar
message of waves and mounds.

I can taste my own desire
writhing between the walls.
The singer is possessed
by the guerilla ghosts
of Wanda Jackson's guitar strap,
Dusty Springfield on ecstasy,
and the coal in little Loretta's dress.
I can hear her clear through the open
door on the edge of last call,
as if she were confined

here with me in this room,
hips cradling a circle above my head
and legs spread akimbo,
edge to edge,
across the foot of my bed.

Through the vision of her voice,
I chart a cockroach crawl
like Descartes in a fever,
the apartment complex becoming a hive,
every room a chamber of vibrating wings,
every wall a comb leaking honey.

II

The girl down the hall is showering,
the last remnants of her love
running down the length of her
thigh on a slow curl of suds.
She's going out tonight to feed
the aching hum left in the wake.
The city crouches around every corner,
licking its neon teeth,
the hall to her next heart
leading straight down its open mouth.

The kid downstairs is cooking up a batch.
He stands shirtless in the parking lot
just outside the corona glow of the streetlight,
the screen of his cell lighting his cruel jaw
and the crossroads of his collarbones blue.
All night, cars pull in and out of the lot.
All night hands slide in and out of pockets,
his parcels blazing in the bludgeoned
eyes of passengers going down.

While I shudder and cough,
hunched and heaving over the porcelain
with dreams of her long, brocade
limbs convulsing in my belly,
her text message tongue
still licking at my ear.

The piston rises and falls,

collapsing my blood and breath,
one of billions burning
in the continual combustion
of the erotic engine of the world.

Cipher

There were all kinds of signs—
cigarette butts in the coffee grounds
spread around the base of her tomatoes,
spiders in the sink
that won't be washed down,
the twists and turns of letters
scrawled at midnight
left in strategic positions around the house,
under the cushions of the couch,
in the refrigerator next to the milk carton,
on Post-it notes folded neatly into the pockets of shirts,
discarded soda cans and beer bottles in the sand,
the water like wet velvet
and all those lonely ribbons of light
igniting the oil refinery
the night you didn't offer her your coat.
But what do you expect from an empty beach at three a.m.?
You might as well have painted the picture yourself
and maybe you did.
But you never really understood what it meant.
You never have.
Only that it all comes down to the banana
ficus that you left on the porch for months
even after she begged you to bring it in.
Its dry, dead leaves falling
over the hardwood floors
the night she screamed,
"Get that goddamn plant in the house before it dies."

Fourth Street Reverie

This week I've eaten four cans of beans
and scraped a few tins of tuna
clean over the kitchen sink,
drank a bottle of whiskey,
ground out five thousand words,
and stumbled along the chain-link
fence outside the school yard.

They forgot to paint the eyes
of the mural on the field house wall.
I text my friend.
Someone has to know.
"...made peace today...
the last handful of dirt...
the other's still outside...
but I like the way the light
falls between the rents..."
There are other words
at the end and in the beginning,
looped around and woven through,
but you get the gist,
or you don't, either way
it's all that's left.

I slip in and out of every spot
on the block, buying four cups
for a dollar at the thrift shop
and a shot on the cuff
from the bartender down the street,
because he owes me
for the time I carried
him home the last night
of the only good woman he'd known,
at least that's the way the song goes
and he's a heap on the couch either way.

Then I'm into the coffee shop
where my cup waits at the register
and the girl with the lonely tattoo
is always starting a new pot.
"He'll be here for a while,"

she says, turning her eyes.
There's only so much
silence a person can take.
Now, she's leaning
her elbows over the counter,
her fists balled up under her chin,
one more wishing for someplace else.
I still haven't found my limit.
Soon I'll be pacing near the bus stop,
smoking cigarettes and mumbling
something about a precipice and dark
water along the rocks, wondering
what eel will raise its back against the waves.

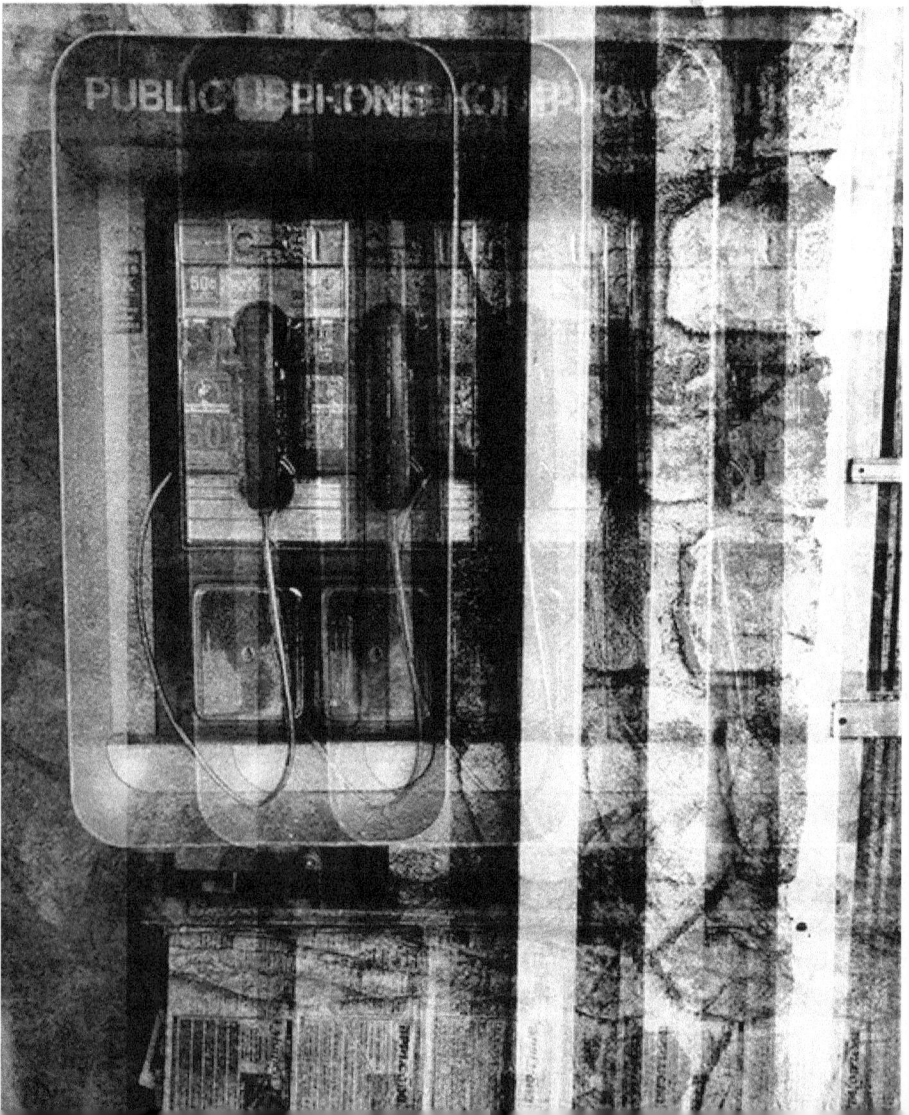

Funny the Things

The girl that seemed to have no palms—
at least no meatiness to them,
the distance from her wrist to her fingers
a smooth, soft line—
spent hundreds of dollars on psychics
and could slap the sense
from your eyes with a single strike.

She loved soups with little pasta stars
and pit bulls and sunflowers—
giant, hulking things in the backyard
that drooped their heads
down to the Mexican tiles
until they fell,
and lie like bodies
waiting for an outline.

We both loved Jack
but she preferred *Five Easy Pieces*
and I've always been partial to *Chinatown*

and he seemed like a decent enough guy,
standing in the doorway with the last box
of her things balanced on his hip.
He shook my hand before he left.
His thin fingers coiled around mine
in the moment before the door closed
left me to the hungry dust
bunnies born of absent furniture and space
I'd have to find some way to fill.

The Lady Says, Vanishing

She has scars on her palms,
stigmata from a prom night crash.
Her date unconscious in his tux,
she was thrown and tried to climb
a chain-link fence on liquid wrists
until the pain flared, red and orange
fireworks along a silver web,
and she had to sit in the wet
until the sirens answered the call.

No fingerprints.
She never leaves
the house without makeup.

In a photograph, she lies
face down on the bed in nothing
but orange panties and a loose barrette.
Dozens of thumbs have left their print,
swirls of oil on her body in miniature.
"I don't take it all that seriously," she says.

For my part, I always tell
the women I meet that I drink.
It makes me seem honest.

Her messages wake me at night.
"If I went missing,
would you look for me?"
When I ask her what
she means, she laughs.
"It's a joke," she says and I wonder
whose hands are on the camera.

I order a beer.
She orders two pints,
a Tequila Sunrise,
and a chaser of chilled
Patrón for the long walk home,
the glass frosted opaque.

"It's closing time," she says
and steps into the crowd
a moment before the music hits.
Slashing behind a spasm of limbs,
she disappears into the sudden
collapse of space.

Drinking Spirits

Bodies pass in pieces
between the bottles
lined along the edge
before the mirrored wall
arms, legs and hips
tussles of hair—
       platinum teased
       frayed and pink
       coarse black
       around the lips and chin
a sailor's arm swings
coiled muscle tattoo
spine spiked Braille
in a backless dress
hairy knuckles splayed
around lip of a glass

Maybe I should get a haircut
       or grow a beard
       or buy a new shirt

Maybe I should burn everything I own

Maybe I should call my mother
       and see about the basement
       or my brother-in-law in Colorado
       (he lives on a ranch)
       or my ex-wife
       or ex-best friend
       or any number
       all the numbers
       and just say, "hello"

Maybe I should dance
       just a little
       lower a heel
       and raise a toe
       so no one would notice
       or as if on a stage—
       a little ball and drag
       a few flowers up my sleeve
       and a rabbit in my hat

Maybe I should tell her that I love her
            or that I don't
            or that I can't
            or that the tortas at the farmers market
            are served with fresh tomatillos
            or that tomorrows
            are just tomorrows
            are just tomorrows
            are just...

Maybe I should slap the guy next to me
            (he looks big)
            or light the napkins on fire
            or throw my glass across the room
            clog the toilets with rolls
            and piss on the floor

Maybe I should scream

Maybe it only takes a little room
            some space to breathe

Maybe on the corner
            under a street light
            the stars cold as fish eyes
            and brilliant as dust

Maybe the frantic flare of her cherry
            the loose smoke
            the coil cradling her cheek
            where my hand should be
                  where is my hand?
                  (in the glass)
                  where is my body bent?
                  (in the glass)
                  where is my face, a white spectral smudge?
                  (in the glass)

Maybe the Cadillac
            long as leviathan
            (river of blood in the glass)
            creeping up around the corner
            the driver just a silhouette
            the headlights two burning gyres

Maybe the kid on his bike
    barreling between us
    (tremble of silver in the glass)
    heading god knows
    maybe east
    maybe west
    maybe straight into oncoming traffic

Maybe the brakes fail
Maybe they don't
Maybe the engine moves on its own
Maybe the neon knows
    (halo of light above the glass)
Maybe me in a high tower
    policing myself into silence
Maybe *I* should go

Or maybe one more
    one more drink
     day
     week
     paycheck
     word
     fuck
     line
     mile on the treadmill
     smile from a stranger
     fist through the wall
Maybe

Bodies pass without pieces
blurred along the lines
the color of milk
liquid light bounding
in a river of light
ghost prints on a cold
window growing warm

Saint Lucy Lost Her Bowl

Saint Lucy brushes against me
as I order another Bushmills,
her eyes in her hands.
She has lost her golden dish.
After all, the Dark Ages
ended in the advent of perspective—
bodies piled on the steps of the Academy,
every face bearded, every hand and finger
curled along the concept of a ground,
save the cracked blue sky between
Adam and the hidden phallus of God.
My favorite Cubism being
the slow slope just below the waist
punctuated by the bone of the hip
and "My mother is a Fish."
This is a mystery
unavailable for digestion
or search engine complicity.
I don't understand these directions.
They don't exist between the bottles
or on my walk back home.
I got her in the corner booth
after I took her hands
and she lifted her skirt so I could see.
There are dimensions curled tighter
than either Michelangelo
or da Vinci could imagine.
This is a mystery.
I like the way they sigh
with their throats between my thumbs
but my mother said a man's feet
were made for standing,
particularly when a woman needs a seat.
"We never really touch," she says.
My hand working like a fulcrum
between her thighs. "It's all
repulsion of electromagnetic fields."
This is a mystery.

The way she covets her breasts
and laughs when I become a child
at the sight of them. Don't even
get me started on the Pre-Raphaelites.
There are too many lilies in that water.
Of course, Botticelli is the best
but my softness lies in the penitent
kneeling beside the bedside
of pornographic swells. Their hearts
and holes plastered to mimic design
along the walls of the next whiskey hall.

After Fern's, the Palms Are Unreal

The moon is a shade
short of full.
There's a long,
tall palm looming
over the iron railing
outside my rented room.

A few hours earlier
at Fern's, a man tells
me the same old story.
She left.

A few months back,
on the same stool,
with her on the opposite side,
she said she was leaving.

I am a stranger to them both.
I only know I've sat between their stories
because they both showed me
the same photo on their phones—
him standing rail straight
with her arms wrapped
around his waist,
her head nestled
just beneath his beard,
both of them smiling
somewhere on a street in Prague.

How do we get here,
after all the miles
between Prague and California?
Funny how we give ourselves without pause,
as if it were preordained,
as if it were necessary,
as if without them palms would not be palms,
as if without their gaze we could not read them.

But they are,
the palms,
there without them,
without us.
There are palms
whether or not
we stand before them
and give the name.

Only the utterances echo,
the garbled dalliances of moths
around a naked bulb,
the false light of a nearly full moon.

You cannot trust light,
never sure whether it's a particle or a wave,
driven through prism labyrinth
reveals the rainbow dissection—
sure, but what is color
but the absorption of all
but a single frequency of light,
a rejection, a pushing away.
Call it green.
Call it red.
Call it gold.
But in the end,
it is the rejection of green,
the rejection of red,
the rejection of gold.
Everything but gold,
but red,
but green—
or the shadow play it offers.

What matters is touch.
The body bends like light,
but what light breaks?
The body breaks.
The body breaks and bends
along the supple column of the spine
to the finger and neck
down to the half-moon hook of the toes.

What matters are the moments
we carve out of each other,
out of the breaking.
This is the land we stand on,
defined by light,
and these are the fingers
we raise to touch the dark
in need of the moon.
Not that cold stone caught by the earth,
but the luminous hole in the night.

I search my phone for photos of Prague
before I realize I've never visited that city
only imagined its ancient skyline.
"Eyes without a face," the radio says.
I touch nothing.
I text instead.
Nothing I mean.
Just words
like bottles climbing a pale
tongue to the moon.

Positioning the Body

"I've always been a beautiful placeholder,"
she said as I lifted her from kitchen floor
and carried her to the back bedroom.
"You know," she said, "the space in-between."

For years, when I was strong,
razor strong—cutting
through the world on quick,
decisive strides—I often thought
of that moment as profound
and even wept, still seeing
the milky curl of her body
in the corner beneath the sink,
the shattered ceramic of the cup
she'd thrown in pieces on dirty linoleum,
beads of tea on the wall,
shining like the cold eyes of fish
between the delicately painted leaves.

Only now, not so strong
or sharp anymore, do I realize
my memory never happened.
I never lifted her.
I've never been that strong.
I came that night to her apartment
with the broken teacup already in my pocket
and dragged her from her bed
to position the body for better light,
lifting the hem of her nightgown
to expose just the right amount of thigh
before placing the shards.
Each drop of tea,
the touch of my finger
on the wall to reflect
the satisfaction of art
well rendered on my face.

Between the Lines

"I miss the way you sigh," I say.

"How do I sigh?" she says,
and I think

like faith to a charismatic,
like fire in a drum,
like lions and tigers and bears, oh my,
like the needle eyes of the succumbed,
like the breaking,
like the body's blood,
like the smell of it eating its way in,
like the sun split open,
like the brilliant dust of stars,
the memory of angels transfixed
along the slope of your thigh,
like numbers,
like the illusion of numbers
breeding themselves along
the contours of your lips,
the final sum,
the answer to 'x,'
all the answers
and all the questions,
like everything,
everything wound and bound
up in the simplest exhalation of breath,
like the final street sign cast in fire,
like loneliness,
like all the people on all the streets
taking one more corner
to the next open door
or the final turn home.

But I say, "I don't know. Heavy."

Snow White in an A-Line Dress

She spends the night thumbing
the edges of old photographs
even after everything has gone digital.
It's not ironic posturing
or some sense of misplaced nostalgia.
It's the feel.

I can tell by the Band-Aid
wrapped tips of her fingers.

I like this about her
and her owl eyes
and the way she sings down the birds
and how she tugs at the hem,
as if she were uncomfortable
with the length of her legs
despite the fact she's the one
who cut the pattern.

Her heart is an open grave
where she tosses every stranger's kiss
since the letter he wrote
said he had no more time
for poison apples or her crystal slumbers
or ragged cabins in the woods
full of jealous dwarves and bitter witches.

"First love is first love," she says,
"is like an egg being cracked.
Once it happens,
the shell is never whole."

And lights a cigarette at the edge,
one long ash breeding between her fingers
before she lets it fall
into the open mouth.
And turns on her heel
away from the spindrift draw of the past
away from the crystal coffin
toward the inevitable lift.
Her lips brushed by the feather of fresh wings,
she leaves her shadow behind,
shimmering at the cemetery gate.

Naucrate's First Flight

I

I read
you were a slave,
read Bruegel's rendering—
limbs flailing,
body cut to pieces,

               t
                h
                  e
                    r
                      o
                        l
                         l
                          a
                  t   d n
            u
          m
        b
       l
      e
of
the
surf

                          foaming
                     at the lip,
                  spitting
              and kissing
sand—
and
          the
            poems
                other
                   men
                      wrote

faced with the Ploughman
foregrounded behind his mare,
wedging a furrow in the earth.

II

I've read a lot,
but I've never read you,

silent   even   in Ovid
like   my own mother
tethered   to   the vacuum in
winter   when   my father died,

                more than black
                Broncos gathered snow.

                                        I rode
                                        the bus
                                        that day.

III

The Fisherman crouches,   The Shepherd and his dog turn away,
absorbed in bait and tackle,   eyes fixed on the point in the sky
unaware of the drowning boy.   where Daedalus once flew—
Does he see fins   now removed by a copyist—
where there are wings?   eyes locked on a bundle of sticks
My father was a fisherman.   loosed by the rocks and waves.
He taught me to cast my line,   This is not Bruegel.
to hunt nightcrawlers   This is not Daedalus.
to farm them in a Folgers can,   The signs are all wrong,
to squat along the water and wait,   lines eroded by more than waves,
only feathers along the lures,   the coasts of continents reassembled
tiny wings to hide the hooks.   to the contours of your invisible face.

IV

Naucrate has come to California
and California has built
its cities to hold her,
wrapped its interstates   around her ankles,
         de   with
         cor   art
         ated   ted   com   mu
         her   in   her   th   mun   se
            ears   pa   face   wi   ity   ums

murals and industrial waste.

Chained on an auction box
at the center   of the city
of angels   where every-
one has   wings but her.
Just as I've   chained her
      in these lines, in the words
                    I cannot unravel,
                       in this offering,
                          written in descent,
                          where I am
                                bound, too.

V

Mother, it's time to go.
Your suitcase packed with mammy dolls,
chickens for sacrifice,
centuries of words
never passed between your teeth
typed clean on white paper.

It won't be easy.
We've slept late,
had to hustle,
gotten lost on the way to the terminal.
The directions didn't lead
where they said they would.

There were black dogs
outside the terminal.
Men in uniform stalked
off with your boarding
pass and passport and I bet
you thought they were never
coming back, that you'd be stuck
on the curb with your bags,
with the taxis pulling up and away,
the traffic circling,
caught in the embrace and release
between the coming and going
until time ran out.

But you made it
through security,
the long lines and bag check,
even after I had to turn
away from security,
to the airport bar
for a few drinks to settle
your nerves before walking
the long hall to the fuselage.

And I can see you now,
nervous at liftoff,
reaching for my hand
and finding the hard
plastic armrest and its useless ashtray,
thinking of contingency plans,
of the distance between your seat
and the emergency exit,
of mechanical error
and loss of flight control
and the lengths you'd go
to return to solid ground
as you lift up
and out
of California.

Boy Cows and Girls

She held the leather
when she slept,
hair fanned in legion
over cotton and linen.
I couldn't help but stand
three fingers deep in the morning,
a collision of rust and sunflower
already gathering at the blinds.

Those days,
we were all in the streets trading hats,
unsure of the difference
between ten gallons and a pillbox.
No one knew the direction downtown
but we were new to our feet
and walking seemed easy,
nothing more natural than motion.
Everything moved after all,
the earth even faster than our feet.

We might have caught the satellite
but there were more angles than angels
in anything the moon had to offer,
and I was left holding the handle,
shaking my head at the sound of wet bristles
despite the ease of letters after midnight.
The day-hardened confetti clumped into pale
shells like calcified snails on the glass.

Often and Again

Often I have dreamt of your elbows
your knees, your back—
the places where the body bends—
and pulled myself from sleep
to light a cigarette and lean
over the iron railing outside my rented room,
littering the patchwork swell
of your body with smoke and ash.

Often I have woken to the sound of sirens
and low flying helicopters,
searchlights blazing through the cracks
in the blinds, circling, illuminating
the broken bodies propped
against cinder block walls
entangled, squatting in the broken
glass strewn across the asphalt,
a pair of feline eyes returning the light,
its body crouched and hidden
beneath a dumpster.

Often I have followed the sound
of my own footfalls,
punch-drunk on memory
and the imaginary lives
of everything and everyone I know,
circling, stuttering my steps to slip
between the cracks in the sidewalk,
searching, kicking at the diamond
piles of glass to send another cat
streaking into the dark,
returning again and again to smoke and ash.

About the Author & Artist

Larry Duncan currently lives in Long Beach, California. In 2012, he received his MFA from California State University, Long Beach. His first chapbook, *Crossroads of Stars and White Lightning*, is available from Arroyo Seco Press.

Ken Oddist Jones is a graphic artist and photographer. He recently relocated to Long Beach by way of Florida where he studied design and studio art at the Florida School of Art. His work was recently featured in *New Legends* and *Then & Now: Conversations with Old Friends*, he was the featured artist of the month on *Cadence Collective*, and he has shown his digital collage work at WE Labs for their third art show, Metamorphosis.

Acknowledgements

The following poems originally appeared in these publications. Many thanks to their respective editors for their support.

"Cipher" *Gutter Eloquence* Issue Twenty-Six
"Fourth Street Reverie" *Dead Snakes*
"Funny the Things" *Electric Windmill Press* Issue 009
"Drinking Spirits" *Horror Sleaze Trash Magazine*
"Saint Lucy Lost Her Bowl" *Carcinogenic Poetry*
"Positioning the Body" *Cultured Vultures*
"Snow White in an A-Line Dress" *Katzenhatz* Bank Heavy Press
"Often and Again" *American Mustard* Volume Two

Also, portions of "Naucrate's First Flight" appeared as "Baby Got Wings" on *The Camel Saloon*

Digital art and photography: p. iii "1888"; p. 3 "Queen of Hearts"; p. 9 "End of the road"; p. 12 "Missed Calls"; p. 15 "Death"; p. 19 "Life and Death"; p. 22 "Studebaker"; p. 27 "Spider Queen"; p. 30 "Transmogrify"; p. 35 "Angel behind the fence"; p. 39 "To anywhere"

www.ingramcontent.com/pod-product-compliance
Lightning Source LLC
Chambersburg PA
CBHW051740040426
42447CB00008B/1233